Editor in Chief
Ina Massler Levin, M.A.

Editor
Eric Migliaccio

Contributing Editor
Sarah Smith

Creative Director
Karen J. Goldfluss, M.S. Ed.

Cover Design
Tony Carrillo / Marilyn Goldberg

Teacher Created Resources, Inc.
12621 Western Avenue
Garden Grove, CA 92841
www.teachercreated.com

ISBN: 978-1-4206-5918-4

©2009 Teacher Created Resources, Inc.
Reprinted, 2019 (PO602461)
Made in U.S.A.

This book belongs to

_____

Ready·Set·Learn

2

Get Ready to Learn!

Get ready, get set, and go! Boost your child's learning with this exciting series of books. Geared to help children practice and master many needed skills, the *Ready·Set·Learn* books are bursting with 64 pages of learning fun. Use these books for . . .

☀ enrichment ☀ skills reinforcement ☀ extra practice

With their smaller size, the *Ready·Set·Learn* books fit easily in children's hands, backpacks, and book bags. All your child needs to get started are pencils, crayons, and colored pencils.

A full sheet of colorful stickers is included. Use these stickers for . . .

☀ decorating pages

☀ rewarding outstanding effort

☀ keeping track of completed pages

Celebrate your child's progress by using these stickers on the reward chart located on the inside cover. The blue-ribbon sticker fits perfectly on the certificate on page 64.

With *Ready·Set·Learn* and a little encouragement, your child will be on the fast track to learning fun!

Aa

Directions: Trace the letters. Color the pictures.

A is for ant.

A is for apple.

A is for ape.

A is for axe.

Color the **A** and the **a**.

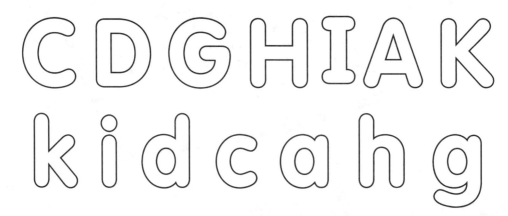

4

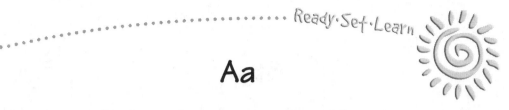

Aa

Directions: Circle each uppercase **A** and lowercase **a** in the box below. Then color the anteater.

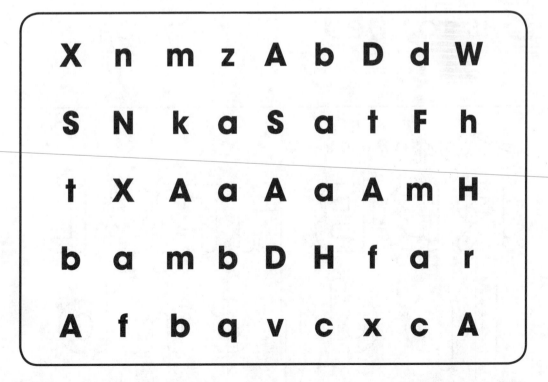

X	n	m	z	A	b	D	d	W
S	N	k	a	S	a	t	F	h
t	X	A	a	A	a	A	m	H
b	a	m	b	D	H	f	a	r
A	f	b	q	v	c	x	c	A

Bb

Directions: Trace the letters. Color the pictures.

B is for bird.

B is for bat.

B is for ball.

B is for bear.

Color the **B** and the **b**.

R D B H P S L
l p d r s h b

Bb

Directions: Color all of the balloons with a **B** on them with a blue crayon. Color all of the balloons with a **b** on them with a brown crayon.

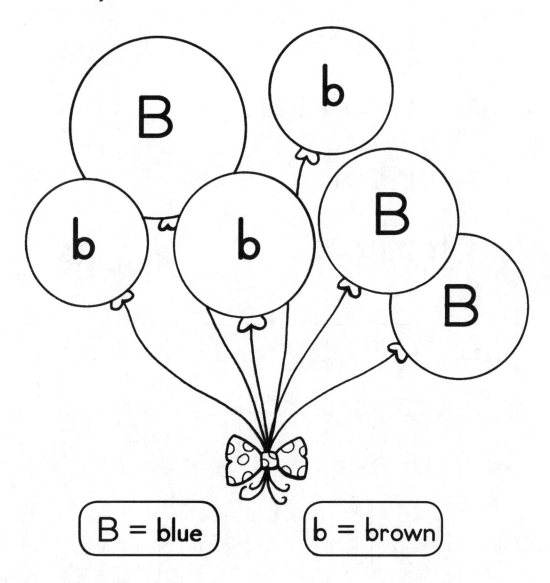

B = blue   b = brown

Cc

Directions: Trace the letters. Color the pictures.

C is for cake.

C is for candle.

C is for cat.

C is for car.

 Color the **C** and the **c**.

DTGCOAR

rotdacg

8

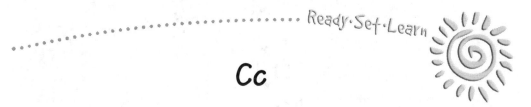

Cc

Directions: Color the **Cc** and the clown. Then find and circle each **C** in the box below.

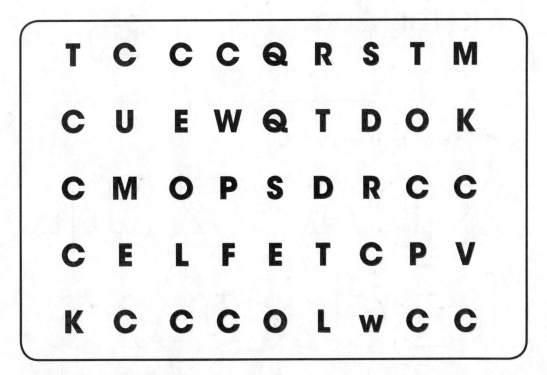

T C C C Q R S T M

C U E W Q T D O K

C M O P S D R C C C

C E L F E T C P V

K C C C O L w C C

Dd

Directions: Trace the letters. Color the pictures.

D is for dinosaur.

D is for dots.

D is for door.

D is for dog.

Color the **D** and the **d**.

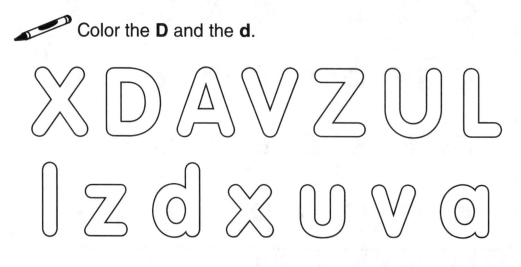

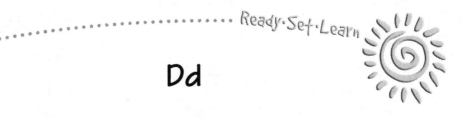

Dd

 Directions: Connect the dots to create the letters **D** and **d**.

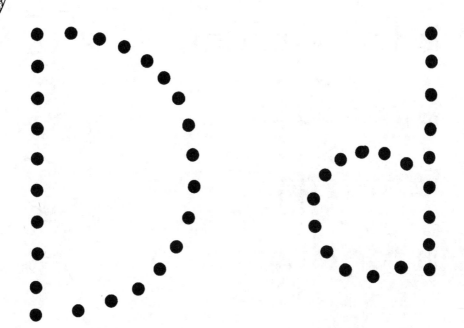

 Draw a picture of something that starts with the letter **d**.

d is for

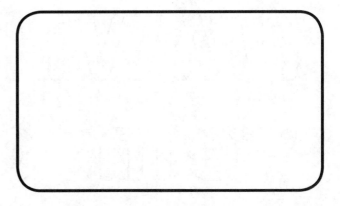

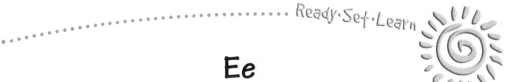

Ee

Directions: Trace the letters. Color the pictures.

E is for elephant.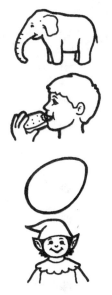

E is for eat.

E is for egg.

E is for elf.

Color the **E** and the **e**.

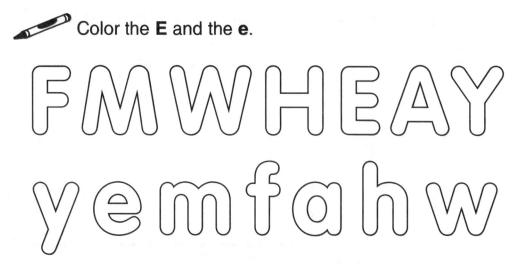

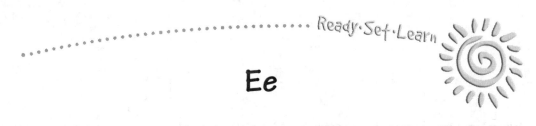

Ee

Directions: Draw a line from each elephant to the letter **E**.

E

E

F

H

E

Ff

Directions: Trace the letters. Color the pictures.

F is for fish.

F is for feather.

F is for fan.

F is for fairy.

Color the **F** and the **f**.

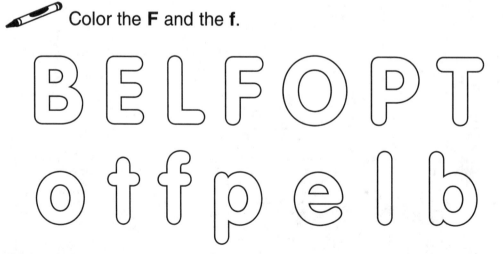

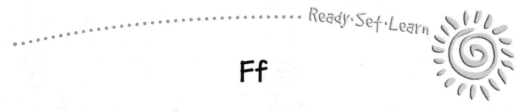

Ff

Directions: Color the shapes that have the letter **f** inside them with your favorite crayon.

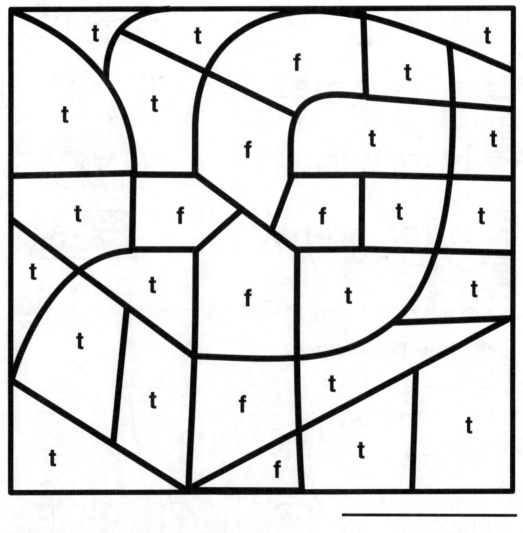

What do you see? Write the letter here. -------

Gg

Directions: Trace the letters. Color the pictures.

G is for garden.

G is for gate.

G is for girl.

G is for game.

Color the **G** and the **g**.

Gg

Directions: Write the beginning letter for each word. Color the pictures.

1. ☐ um

2. ☐ oat

3. ☐ as

Directions: Practice printing the letter **g**.

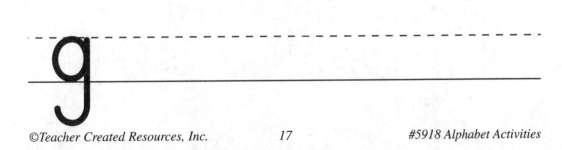

Hh

Directions: Trace the letters. Color the pictures.

H is for house.

H is for hill.

H is for hat.

H is for hand.

Color the **H** and the **h**.

VBHRTUS
trbhvsu

18

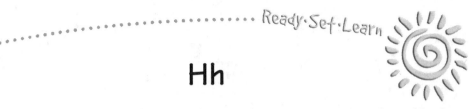

Hh

Directions: Color the pictures in the heart that begin with the letter **h**.

Ii

Directions: Trace the letters. Color the pictures.

I is for insect.

I is for ice cream.

I is for inch.

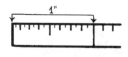

I is for ice.

Color the **I** and the **i**.

Ii

Directions: Color the I's and the ice cream. Find and circle each uppercase **I** and lowercase **i** in the box below.

L	i	I	i	v	n	O	u	m
E	x	i	Q	r	e	k	c	i
T	o	I	n	n	m	D	d	s
C	L	I	p	o	M	t	z	i
Z	I	i	i	I	w	o	w	d	I

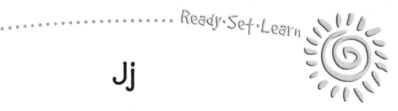

Jj

Directions: Trace the letters. Color the pictures.

J is for jellybeans.

J is for jar.

J is for jump rope.

J is for jet.

Color the **J** and the **j**.

Jj

Directions: Color each shape that has an uppercase **J** with a yellow crayon. Color each shape that has an lower-case **j** with a black crayon.

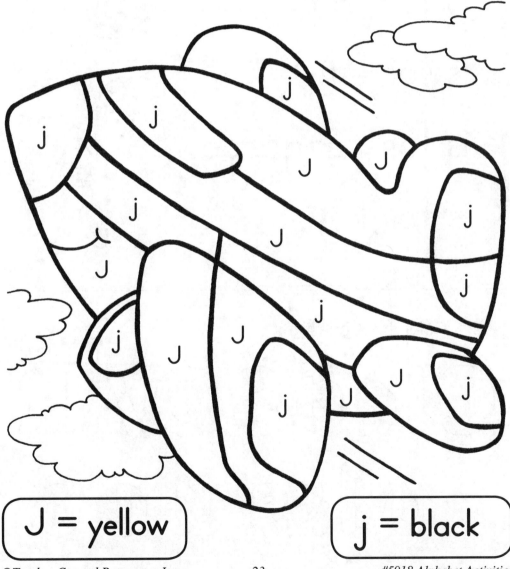

J = yellow

j = black

Kk

Directions: Trace the letters. Color the pictures.

K is for king.

K is for kite.

K is for kangaroo.

K is for key.

Color the **K** and the **k**.

Kk

Directions: Color each ball with an uppercase **K** yellow. Color each ball with a lowercase **k** red.

Ll

Directions: Trace the letters. Color the pictures.

L is for lizard.

L is for leopard.

L is for ladder.

L is for lemonade.

Color the **L** and the **l**.

XDAVZUL

l z d x u v a

26   ©Teacher Created Resources, Inc.

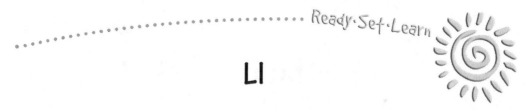

LI

Directions: Color the objects in the picture that begin with **I**.

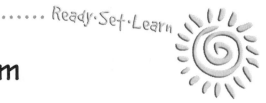

Mm

Directions: Trace the letters. Color the pictures.

M is for mountain.

M is for moon.

M is for magnet.

M is for mitten.

Color the **M** and the **m**.

FMWHNAY

ynmfahw

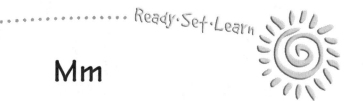
Mm

Directions: Draw a line from each picture that starts with **m** to a mailbox.

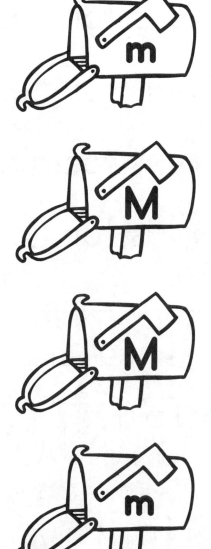

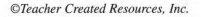

Nn

Directions: Trace the letters. Color the pictures.

N is for needle.

N is for nest.

N is for nine.

N is for neck.

Color the **N** and the **n**.

RNWFMPV

m v f p n w r

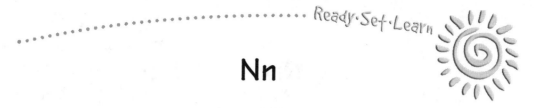

Nn

Directions: Color each nut that has an **N** or **n** inside. Then color the squirrel.

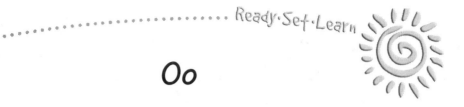

Oo

Directions: Trace the letters. Color the pictures.

O is for octopus.

O is for orange.

O is for olive.

O is for otter.

Color the **O** and the **o**.

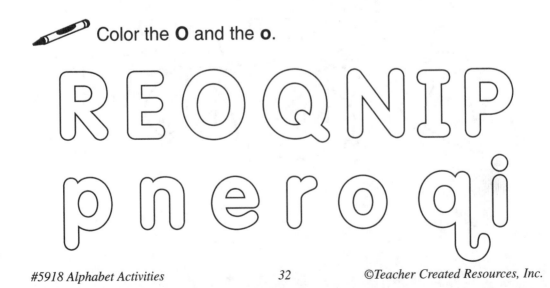

32

Oo

Directions: Color each circle with an **O** orange.

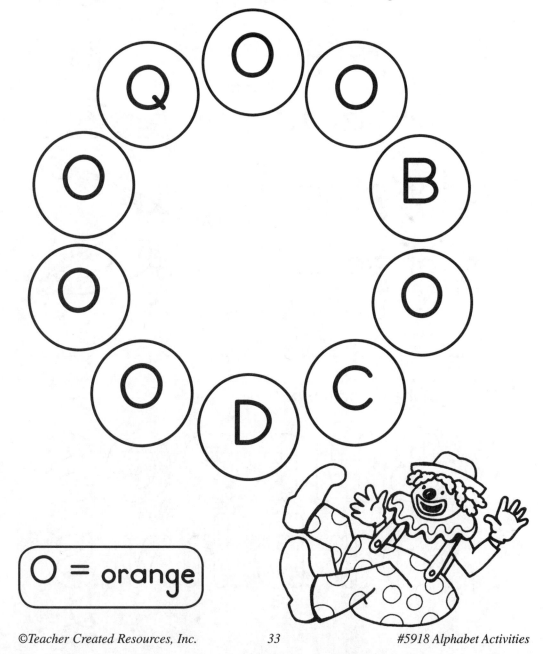

O = orange

Pp

Directions: Trace the letters. Color the pictures.

P is for penguin.

P is for pizza.

P is for pencil.

P is for peas.

Color the **P** and the **p**.

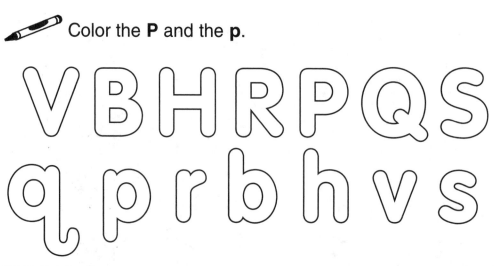

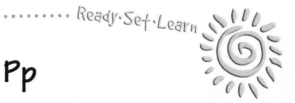
Pp

Directions: Practice making an uppercase **P** and a lowercase **p** inside the big pencil. Color the pencils that have words that begin with the /p/ sound, as in *pencil*.

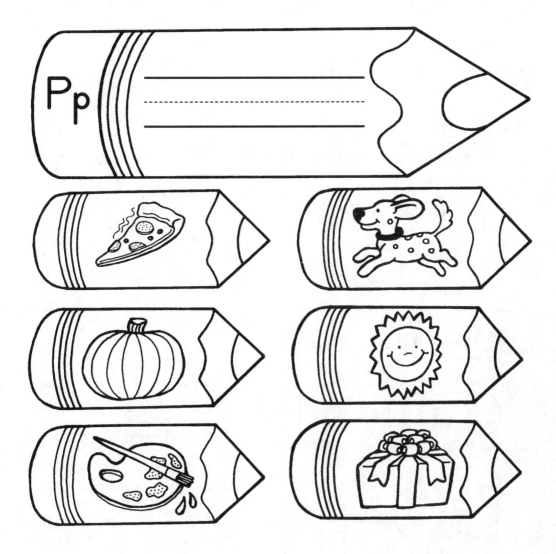

Qq

Directions: Trace the letters. Color the pictures.

Q is for queen.

Q is for quilt.

Q is for question mark.

Q is for quiet.

Color the **Q** and the **q**.

CQGHPAD

dpqcahg

36

Qq

Directions: Trace the line from the uppercase **Q** to the lowercase **q**. Make a quilt. Color each uppercase **Q** green. Color each lowercase **q** yellow.

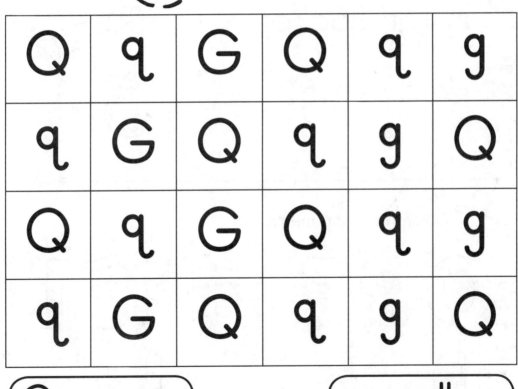

Q = green

q = yellow

Rr

Directions: Trace the letters. Color the pictures.

R is for rainbow.

R is for ruler.

R is for rocket.

R is for ring.

Color the **R** and the **r**.

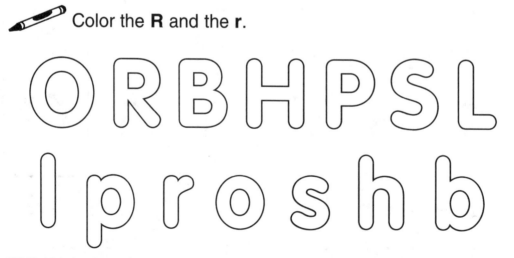

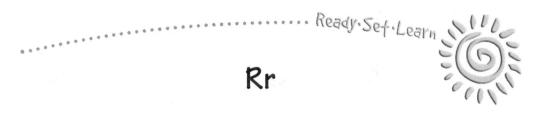

Rr

Directions: Color the objects in the picture that begin with **r**.

Ss

Directions: Trace the letters. Color the pictures.

S is for **s**and.

S is for **s**ailboat.

S is for **s**ea.

S is for **s**un.

Color the **S** and the **s**.

DOGCSER

rsodecg

Ss

Directions: Look at the pictures. Color the pictures that start with the /s/ sound, as in *sun*.

Tt

Directions: Trace the letters. Color the pictures.

T is for turtle.

T is for truck.

T is for tent.

T is for tree.

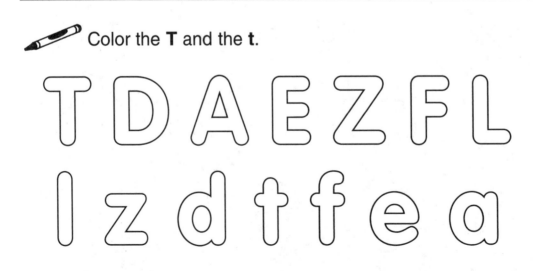

Color the **T** and the **t**.

TDAEZFL

lzdtfea

42

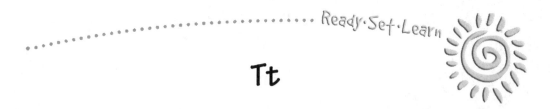
Tt

Directions: Color the pictures in the turtle that begin with the letter **t**.

Uu

Directions: Trace the letters. Color the pictures.

U is for **u**mbrella.

U is for **u**pside-down.

U is for **u**nder.

U is for **u**p.

Color the **U** and the **u**.

Uu

Directions: Color each raindrop that has a lowercase **u** blue. Color the other raindrops green.

Vv

Directions: Trace the letters. Color the pictures.

V is for volcano.

V is for vase.

V is for violet.

V is for vest.

Color the **V** and the **v**.

NVAFOWY
oyfwvan

Vv

Directions: Trace the lines from the uppercase **V** to the lowercase **v**. Color each **v** and the vase of violets below.

Ww

Directions: Trace the letters. Color the pictures.

W is for wagon.

W is for window.

W is for watermelon.

W is for worm.

Color the **W** and the **w**.

LWYSNMV

mnwlvsy

48

Ww

Directions: Color the objects in the picture below that begin with **w**.

Xx

Directions: Trace the letters. Color the pictures.

X is for **x**-ray.

X is for e**x**it.

X is for e**x**am.

X is for **x**ylophone.

Color the **X** and the **x**.

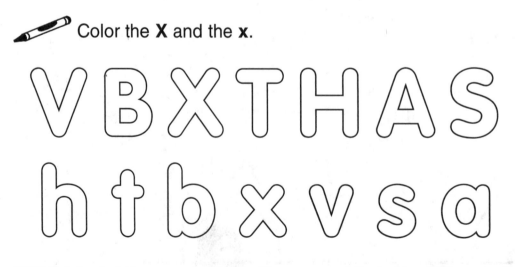

50

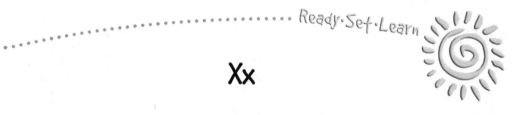

Xx

Directions: Put an **X** on each place on the map that is marked with a spot.

Yy

Directions: Trace the letters. Color the pictures.

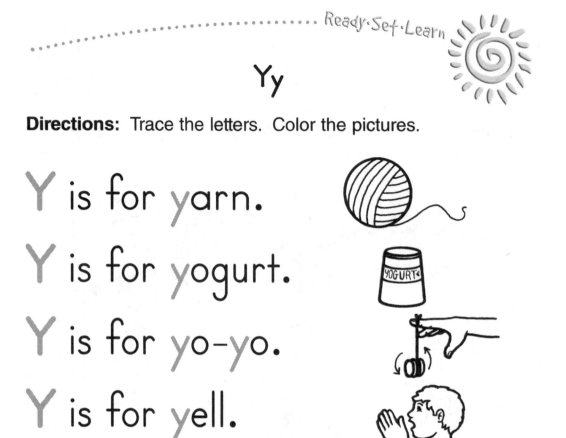

Y is for yarn.

Y is for yogurt.

Y is for yo-yo.

Y is for yell.

Color the **Y** and the **y**.

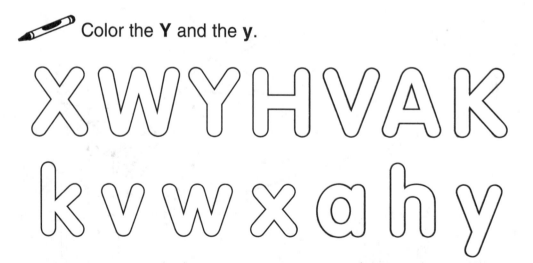

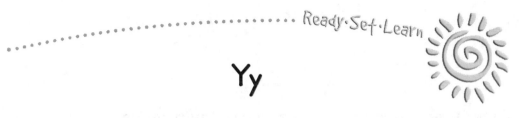

Yy

Directions: Look at Yolanda's yard. Color each hidden **Y** in the yard green.

Zz

Directions: Trace the letters. Color the pictures.

Z is for zipper.

Z is for zebra.

Z is for zero.

Z is for zoo.

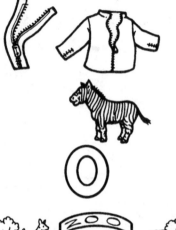

Color the **Z** and the **z**.

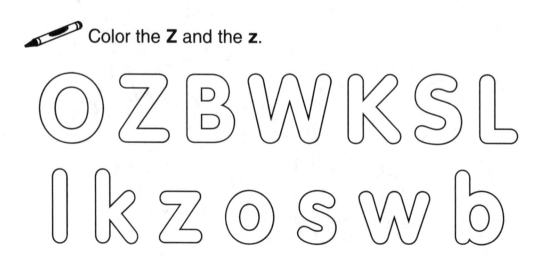

Zz

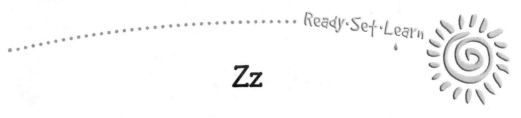

Directions: Write the beginning sound for each word.

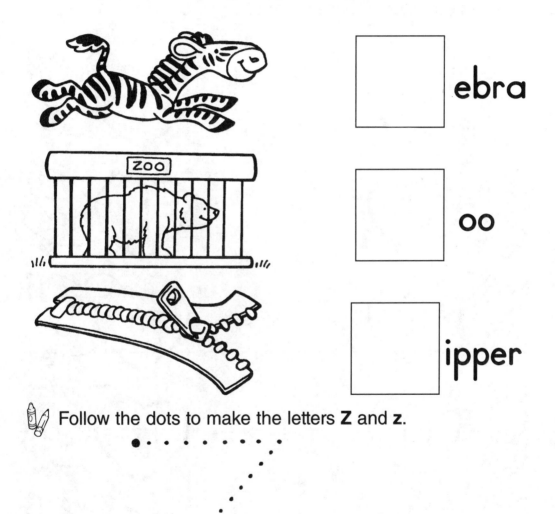

ebra

oo

ipper

Follow the dots to make the letters **Z** and **z**.

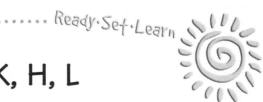

M, J, K, H, L

Directions: Draw a line from each lowercase letter to its uppercase partner. Color the birds.

N, P, Q, R, S

Directions: Draw a line from each uppercase letter to its lowercase partner. Color the matching apples the same color.

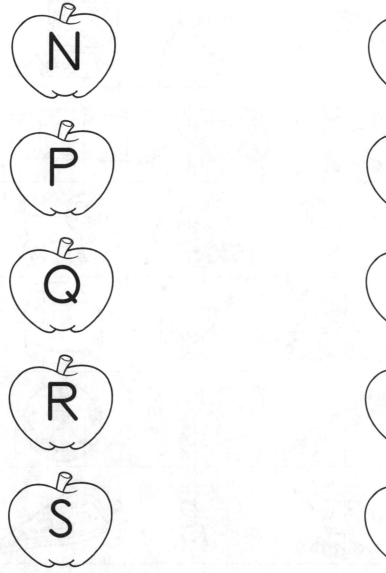

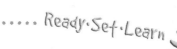

C, D, F, J, K, R

Directions: Color the picture in the row that starts with the letter.

L, B, G, H, T, M

Directions: Color the picture in the row that starts with the letter.

A-Z

Directions: Connect the letters A-Z to see the picture.

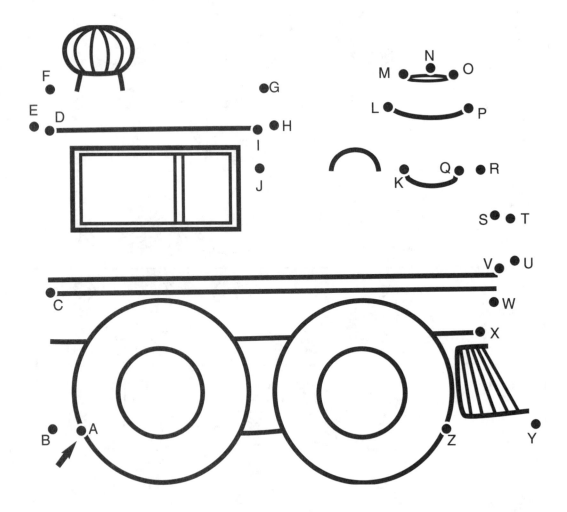

The Birthday Party

Directions: Allie's friends all brought capital-letter gifts to her birthday party. They hid them throughout the room. Help Allie find her gifts. Circle the letters you find.

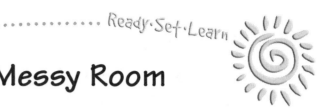

The Messy Room

Directions: Jason spilled his box of lowercase letters in his room. Help Jason find his lowercase letters. Circle the ones you find.

This Award
Is Presented To

_____

FOR

★ Doing Your Best

★ Trying Hard

★ Not Giving Up

★ Making a
Great Effort

64